People and Nature

Program Authors

Connie Juel, Ph.D.

Jeanne R. Paratore, Ed.D.

Deborah Simmons, Ph.D.

Sharon Vaughn, Ph.D.

PEARSON

Scott
Foresman

Glenview, Illinois
Boston, Massachusetts
Chandler, Arizona
Upper Saddle River, New Jersey

ISBN-13: 978-0-328-45282-8
ISBN-10:   0-328-45282-3

8 9 10 V011 14 13
CC1

UNIT 3 Contents

People and Nature

Green Thumbs in Action

Contents

Green Thumbs in Action

Words 2 the Wise

Gardens have been around for a long time. Why do so many people like them? Think about this as you read.

Let's Explore

Gardens

People around the world like gardens. Gardens are nice to look at. We can visit a few gardens now. That will help us see what can grow in a garden.

Vegetable Gardens

Yummy things to eat grow in some gardens. Which vegetables do you like? Corn? Beans? Peas? You can grow them in a vegetable garden. People plant these gardens to get fresh vegetables and feed their families. Many people plant vegetables in spring. Then they can eat fresh vegetables all summer long.

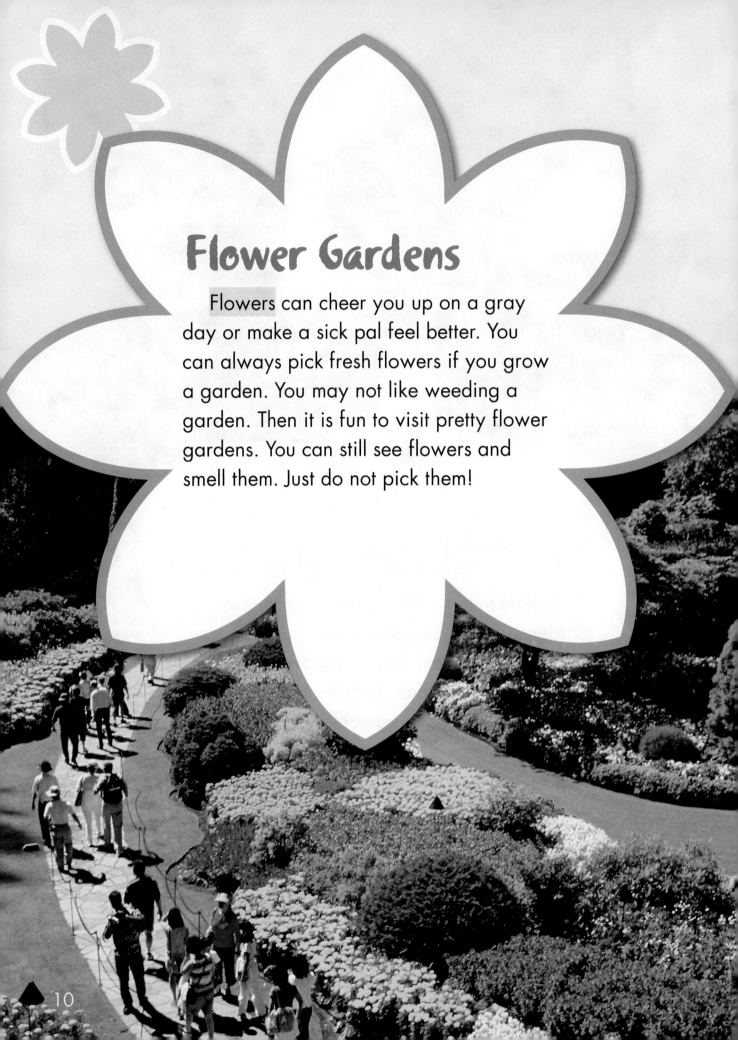

Flower Gardens

Flowers can cheer you up on a gray day or make a sick pal feel better. You can always pick fresh flowers if you grow a garden. You may not like weeding a garden. Then it is fun to visit pretty flower gardens. You can still see flowers and smell them. Just do not pick them!

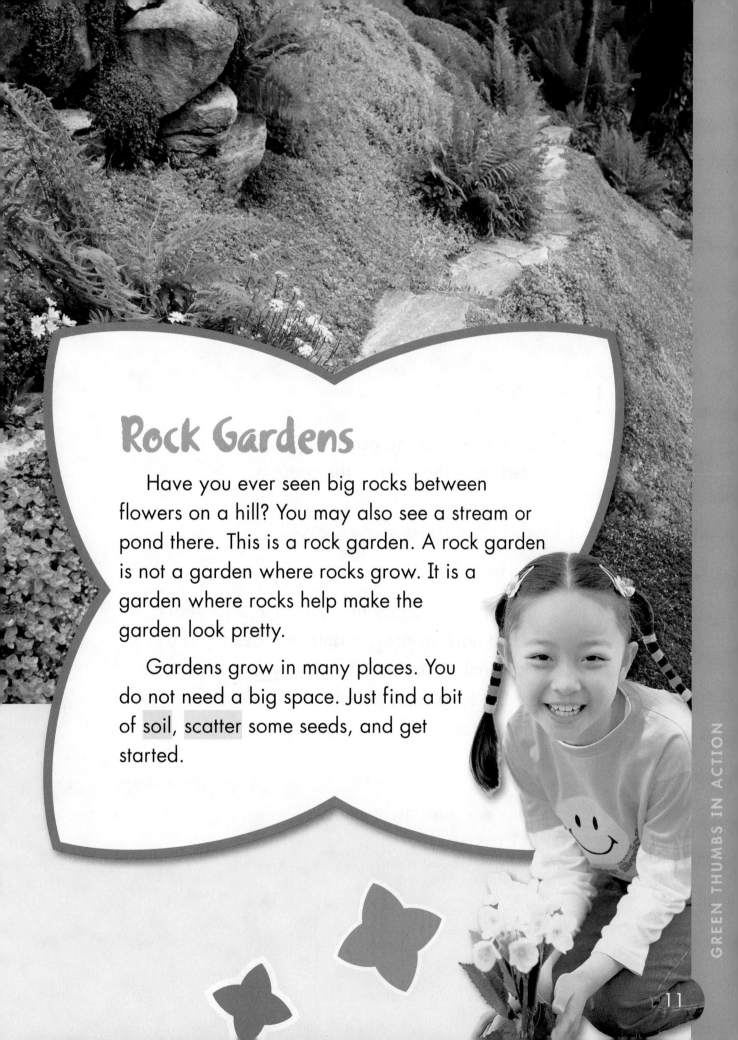

Rock Gardens

Have you ever seen big rocks between flowers on a hill? You may also see a stream or pond there. This is a rock garden. A rock garden is not a garden where rocks grow. It is a garden where rocks help make the garden look pretty.

Gardens grow in many places. You do not need a big space. Just find a bit of soil, scatter some seeds, and get started.

GARDENS
Past and Present

by Bret Allan

Let's look at some gardens people have planted from the past to the present.

The Hanging Gardens of Babylon*

Babylon was a city in a desert 2,500 years ago. It is hard to grow plants in a desert. The soil isn't rich.** The weather is dry. It doesn't rain much. But long ago, people in that desert made gardens grow.

*Babylon (BAB-uh-lon) This city from long ago was on land that is now part of the country of Iraq.

**rich good for growing plants

12

How did they do it? They put the Hanging Gardens on the banks, or sides, of a river. And they planted them on different levels.* Ropes lifted buckets of water from the river up to the top level. Then the water ran down to other levels. That's how the plants got plenty of water.

Many people back then wrote about these gardens. That is why we know about them today.

*__levels__ layers or steps

The Floating Gardens of Xochimilco (so-chee-MEEL-ko)

Aztec people lived in Mexico City more than 500 years ago. Much of their land was marsh* land. It was too wet for crops to grow. The Aztec people fixed this problem by making land in the marshes. They dug up mud from a marsh and piled it in long, wide piles. They mixed marsh plants in with the mud. This made rich soil that was perfect for planting flowers and vegetables such as beans.

*marsh low land that never dries out

14

Aztec people often made homes on these piles of soil. This made it easy for them to tend* crops. It was also easy to keep the soil wet with marsh water so close by. Today people still grow flowers and vegetables for Mexico City in these gardens.

*tend care for

Monticello*

Thomas Jefferson was one of the first leaders of our country. He was our third president. But Jefferson also liked growing a garden. Jefferson made notes that tell us what his garden was like. He planted flowers and plants from all over the world.

*Monticello (mon-tuh-CHEL-o) Thomas Jefferson's home in Virginia

Jefferson planted more than 150 kinds of apples, peaches, and grapes. His gardens held 300 kinds of vegetables. And did you know that Jefferson really liked peas a lot? In his garden, he had fifteen kinds of peas!

People still visit his home and gardens. They can learn what gardens were like in Jefferson's day.

The Edible Schoolyard

At Martin Luther King Junior Middle School in California, there's a huge garden. The kids in that school learn how to plant seeds, take care of plants, and then harvest the crops. Working in this garden helps kids learn how to grow the things we eat.

When it's time to pick the vegetables, there are yummy things, like peas, to snack on. But their work isn't over yet. Next, the kids use vegetables from the garden to prepare meals. Then they eat the meal together. When lunch is over, the scraps go back in the soil. This keeps the soil rich for next year's garden.

What Do You Think?

In the gardens you read about, what steps did people take to grow their flowers and vegetables?

Belle

by Rachel Sills • illustrated by Mercedes McDonald

Long ago in a place far away, some very dull people lived in a very dull and very drab land.

"What can we do today?" Neal asked.

"I don't know. What can we do?" asked Bree.

Neal answered, "I don't know. . . z-z-z-z." And he went to sleep. People slept a lot in this dull, drab land. That's how dull it was.

The soil in this land was muddy and gray. Flowers were drab and gray. Vegetables were dull and gray. The sky was foggy and gray. Boys and girls had no color. They didn't even know what color was. How did this happen? No one knows. It just did.

So life went on in this dull, drab, gray land.

21

One day, the people spotted a new girl. This girl didn't look like them. She didn't act like them. In fact, she had lots of life, and she had lots of color. People hadn't ever seen a girl like her before. Her eyes were as blue as the sky. Not their sky, of course. Her hair was as red as a rose. Not their roses, of course.

People began calling her Belle, because all day long she sang about blue bells and pretty shells. As she sang, she skipped over dull, gray farms. She went up drab, gray hills. She hopped over muddy ditches. And she scattered tiny things. What were they? What did she scatter on the soil? No one knew.

People asked Belle where she came from. But she just smiled. They asked what she was scattering. But she just smiled even more. Then, one day she left, just as fast as she had come. And in a short time, those dull people forgot her.

A year passed. The land was still gray. Flowers were still drab. Vegetables were still dull. The sky was still foggy and gray.

But one day, a change came. Tiny green plants started growing in the soil. They sprang up on the farms. They popped up on the hills. They burst up in the ditches.

"What's happening? Nothing looks the same! The hills are covered with green! The farms have green carpets! Even the trees are turning green!" cried Neal and Bree.

Then one day, the biggest surprise of all happened. People woke up and saw flowers in every color! There were yellow daisies and red poppies and blue flax. There were white lilies and pink asters and black-eyed Susans.

Where had these colors come from? It was Belle. Where had she gone? No one knew. But they knew she had scattered those colors.

That place began to change more and more. The sky turned blue, and the sun shone yellow. The land wasn't dull any more, so the people weren't dull. They smiled at each other and spoke of many things. They began growing more vegetables and even more flowers. And no one went to sleep in the day. There was too much to do. Now they had to scatter colors just as Belle had.

What Do You Think?

How did the land change in the story?

In the Kitchen

When you plant a garden, you can use the vegetables you grow in tasty recipes. This is a recipe the students at Martin Luther King Junior Middle School make with their garden vegetables.

Frittata

8 eggs, well beaten

2–3 cups assorted vegetables and herbs (any of these vegetables: chard, thyme, parsley, spinach, cooked potatoes, garlic, onion, tomato, basil, mushrooms—things you like!)

½ cup grated cheese

2 Tablespoons olive oil

Crack the eggs into a mixing bowl and beat well using a whisk. Wash and chop all vegetables and herbs. Heat olive oil in a skillet. Add the chopped herbs and vegetables and cook until slightly tender. Add the eggs and cheese, stirring well. Cook till eggs are halfway cooked. Finish in a hot oven (400°F) till puffy and golden brown and eggs are set. Time to eat!!!

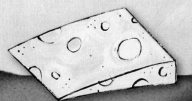

4YOU2Do

Word Play

Can you name more flowers or vegetables? Make a list of each to find out.

Making Connections

People in Babylon planted gardens in the desert. Aztec people planted crops in marshes. Belle planted pretty plants in a drab, dull land. How did each of them make the land better?

On Paper

You read about many different gardens. Which one would you most like to visit? Write about it. Tell what you think is special about it.

Possible answers to Word Play: Flowers—violet, buttercup, mum, rose, tulip; Vegetables—beets, carrots, lettuce, peas, onions

NATURE
•The True Story•

Contents

NATURE
•The True Story•

Words 2 the Wise

Nature has some secrets to share. What can they be? As you read, find out about **Nature: The True Story.**

Secrets of Nature

What is a rainbow? Why do seasons change? What makes thunder? In the past, people did not know. They made up tales called myths to explain things in nature. Since those days, scientists have discovered why these things happen.

What is a rainbow?

Myth Long ago, a Greek myth tried to explain rainbows. Iris was the Greek goddess of rainbows. Iris used a rainbow as a road. Her rainbow went between her home in the sky and Earth.

Fact Scientists know that real rainbows form when sun shines on water droplets in the air. Water bends the sun's rays. That makes them split into colors.

Why do seasons change?

Myth Demeter (di-MEE-ter) was the Greek goddess of plants. She had a child who was kidnapped. Crops stopped growing because she was so sad. This was winter. When her child came back, Demeter let spring return.

Fact The Earth is tilted. When places on Earth are tilted toward the sun, it is summer. When places on Earth are tilted away from the sun, it is winter.

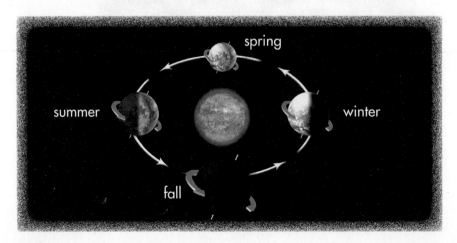

What makes thunder?

Myth In a Norse* myth, Thor was the god of thunder. Thor rode across the sky in a cart pulled by goats. When Thor tossed his huge hammer, it flashed and made thunder.

*__Norse__ Norse myths came from Scandinavia long ago. Sweden, Norway, and Denmark are in Scandinavia.

Fact Scientists know how storms with thunder form. At times, cold air clashes with warm, wet air. When that happens, it makes storms and thunder.

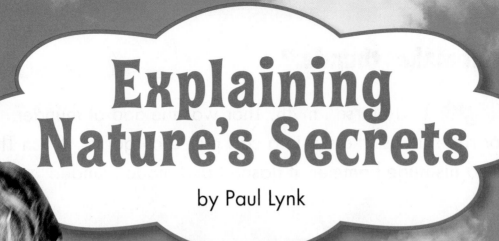

Explaining Nature's Secrets

by Paul Lynk

We've all seen nature at work. Plants and animals grow and change. Let's see how scientists explain some secrets of nature to us.

Me and My Shadow

Is your shadow long or short? You've seen it both ways. How can that be? Scientists get the answer from the sun. Shadows form when something blocks the sun's rays.

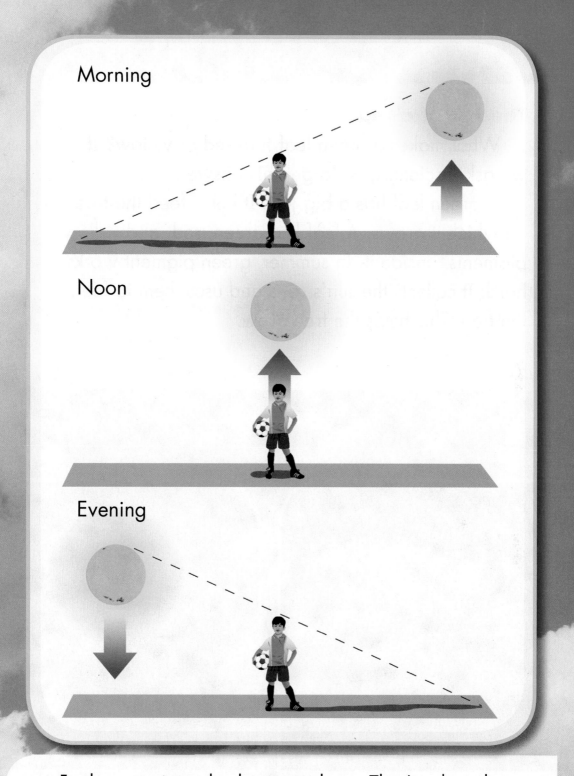

Morning

Noon

Evening

In the morning, shadows are long. That's when the sun is just rising. It is still low in the sky.

At lunch time, shadows are short. The sun shines straight down on us.

Late in the day, shadows are long again. The sun is setting. It is low in the sky again.

The Job of a Leaf

What makes a green leaf turn red or yellow? If we ask a scientist, we'd get this answer.

A green leaf has a big job. It helps feed the tree on which it grows. A leaf has green, red, and yellow pigments* inside it. In summer, green pigment works hard. It collects the sun's rays and uses them to feed the tree. This helps the tree grow.

Spring Leaves bud out. The tree begins growing again.

Summer Green pigment collects the sun's rays. The tree grows.

***pigment** the part of a living thing that gives it its color

40

In winter, the tree needs to rest. It doesn't need to grow for a while. So it doesn't need to be fed. The green pigment fades. The yellow and red pigments take over. Then nature gives us a show of color just before winter starts.

Fall The tree gets ready to rest. Red and yellow pigments take over.

Winter The tree rests during winter.

Secrets in a Tree Trunk

We know that trees grow each year, but a tree can't tell us its age. We can discover a tree's age only after it's been cut down. Scientists use growth rings in a tree trunk to discover a tree's age.

Look at a tree stump, and you'll see growth rings. Each ring stands for one year of growing. How many rings are there? That's the tree's age.

tree rings

Tree rings can also tell us about the climate in the past. A thick tree ring means the tree had plenty of rain and sun that year. A thin tree ring means that weather was bad or that insects or fire harmed the tree.

tree rings

Music Class for Birds

Did you know that birds must learn to sing? Scientists say baby birds first listen to grown-up birds. They try to sing what they hear. At first, their singing is more like screeching. That's because they're still learning. But they keep trying! Some scientists think baby birds dream about singing. Their dreams may help them learn their songs.

More Work to Do

Nature has lots more secrets. Scientists keep discovering them. They're trying to explain our world to us with facts. These days we don't need myths to understand nature. We can find out nature's secrets from scientists.

What Do You Think?

What are some secrets of nature that scientists have explained to us?

Scientists at Work

by Lindy Russell

You've read about things in nature that scientists can explain to us. Scientists have many different jobs. Let's take a look at some of them.

Scientists Who Study Plants

Some scientists study plants that we eat. They try to make plants that grow better. Their goal is to produce plenty of good crops to feed us well.

A scientist who studies plants is a botanist (BOT-uhn-ist).

Some scientists study plants to find cures for sick people. Many plants can help the sick. These scientists find out which plants can save lives.

Heart medicine comes from foxglove plants.

Scientists Who Study Animals

If you'd like to study animals, these jobs are for you. From tiny bugs to huge whales, there are plenty of animals to study.

Some scientists study insects, such as bees, that help us. These insects make things we use. Scientists who study these insects focus* on getting them to produce more of what we use.

*focus to pay close attention to something

A scientist who studies insects is an entomologist (en-tuh-MOL-uh-jist).

Other insects can harm us and make us sick. Insects can eat crops and kill plants. Scientists study ways to prevent these problems.

If you'd like working with bigger animals, you may like being a vet. Some vets help pets. Other vets treat farm animals or wild animals. Vets help keep animals in good shape. Vets help sick or injured animals get better.

A doctor who treats animals is a veterinarian (vet-er-uh-NAIR-ee-uhn).

Scientists Who Study Fossils

Some scientists study the history of life on Earth. These scientists study fossils of plants and animals. Fossils are remains or marks left by living things from long ago.

A scientist who studies fossils is a paleontologist (pay-lee-on-TOL-uh-jist).

A fossil can be a bone, or it can be the shape that an animal or plant left in a rock. Scientists who study fossils have discovered extinct animals, such as T. Rex, that aren't living now. Plant fossils help scientists discover what the climate was like on Earth long ago. These facts can help predict what may happen to our climate.

Scientists Who Study Weather

What will the weather be this week? Hot and sunny? Wet and rainy? Cold and snowy? Some scientists forecast* the weather.

People depend on weather forecasts. We use them to plan events such as picnics. Pilots use them to decide if it is safe to fly. Farmers use them to know if they must protect their crops from frost.

*forecast to tell what is going to happen

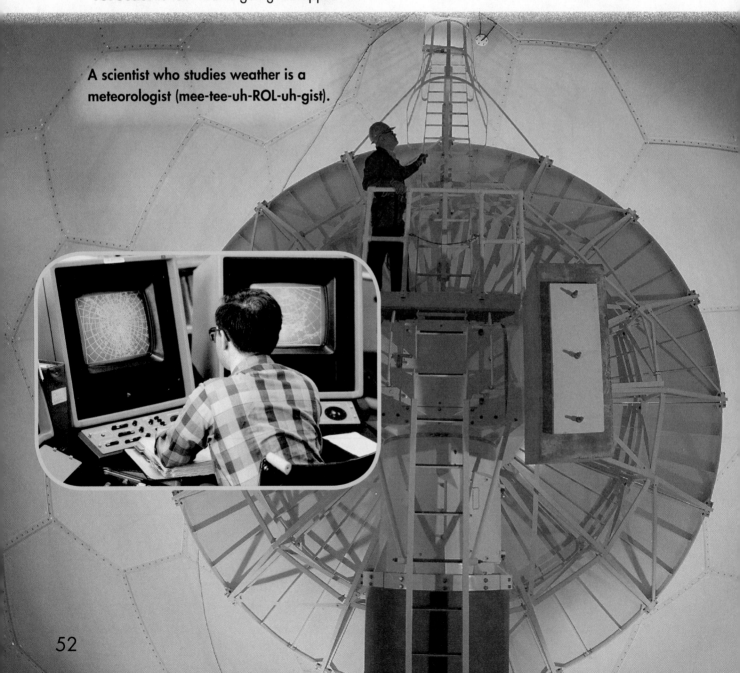

A scientist who studies weather is a meteorologist (mee-tee-uh-ROL-uh-gist).

Scientists who forecast weather use modern tools. Radar* detects, or spots, storms, strong winds, or other bad weather. Warning people about bad storms, such as tornadoes (tor-NAY-dohz), can save lives. People can take shelter or get out of the storm's path.

These scientists do important jobs. We're so glad that we can depend on them to tell us how nature works.

*radar a tool that uses radio waves to find unseen objects

What Do You Think?
Scientists have many different jobs.
Tell why their jobs are important

Why Owl Hunts at Night

a Tale from Puerto Rico
illustrated by Felipe Ugalde

Everyone knows that owls hunt only at night. But long ago owls hunted only by day! They had no feathers, so they needed the sun to keep them warm.

One night the birds decided to have a big party. But Owl said, "I can't go out at night. It's chilly, and I've no feathers to keep me warm."

Eagle said, "You're right. I have an idea! We can each loan you a feather. Then you'd be warm."

All the birds loaned Owl some feathers. "You must return them tomorrow," Eagle told Owl.

54

Owl looked beautiful in his friends' feathers! He had a wonderful time at the party. And, for a change, he felt warm. As it grew late, Owl thought about returning the feathers. But he didn't want to be cold and plain ever again. Just before the party ended, Owl flew away.

The next day all the birds tried to find Owl. They're still looking to this very day. And that is why Owl comes out only at night. He knows that other birds sleep at night. And he doesn't want to give back his warm, beautiful feathers.

4 YOU 2 DO

Word Play

How much do you know about scientists? Make a word web for the word **scientist** to find out. Can you include all these words in your web?

discover   environment   problem
weather   nature   solution

scientist

Making Connections

Which kind of scientist studies thunder? tree rings? why leaves change color? how birds learn to sing?

On Paper

If you were a scientist, what would you want to study in nature? Write about it and tell why it interests you.

A CLOSER LOOK

Contents

A CLOSER LOOK

Words 2 the Wise

We can use our senses to learn more about nature. As you read, think about what nature can teach us when we take **a closer look.**

Using Our Senses

Our five senses are sight, smell, hearing, touch, and taste. We can use our five senses to help us learn about nature.

You're in school now. But let's pretend we're on a forest trail. What will we discover when we use our senses?

Sight In a forest we will see trees, right? What kind do you think we'll see? Is sunshine shining on their branches? Will we spot a butterfly or a toad? Maybe we'll see a deer.

Smell Let's take a big whiff. What can we smell? Can we smell wildflowers that grow here? Pine trees? A skunk? How would that smell?

Hearing Stop and listen. What can we hear? Is a
bluebird chirping nearby? Are insects buzzing? Perhaps a
classmate is speaking. Shhh, let's listen to the forest.

Touch Now you've picked up a pinecone. Do you like
how it feels? Let's touch some moss* on a tree. Is it soft or
scratchy?

*moss small green plants that grow close together

Taste Perhaps this forest has an apple tree. Shall we taste an apple? No, we'd better let the birds eat them.

We're using our senses every moment of every day. Use your senses on your trip home today. What will you see, smell, hear, touch, or taste?

A Lesson from Mother Nature

by Phyllis Perry

Scientists use their senses of taste, touch, hearing, sight, and smell. They need them to observe nature. Nature might help them get some grand ideas.

Leonardo da Vinci (lee-uh-NARD-oh duh VIN-chee)

The great artist Leonardo da Vinci lived long ago. This man was a scientist as well as an artist. He spent days observing birds in flight. This sight made him wonder how a bird flies.

Leonardo sketched birds taking off and landing. Birds use wings to fly. How do birds' wings work? Could men fly with wings too? Leonardo sketched his ideas for flying machines. Leonardo never made a flying machine that worked. But later his ideas helped people build airplanes and gliders.*

*gliders light airplanes with no engines

Sir Isaac Newton (EYE-zuhk NOOT-n)

Have you ever gotten big ideas while resting? That's what happened to Sir Isaac Newton. About 300 years ago, he had a taste for an apple. While he sat outside by an apple tree, an apple fell next to him. This sight made him start to think. Why did that apple go down and not up or to the side?

Isaac decided a special force must be pulling the apple to earth. He named that pulling force *gravity.* Gravity doesn't work just on apples. People are held on Earth by this force too. In fact, gravity works on everything. The bigger something is, the more gravity pulls on it.

Joseph Glidden

About 150 years ago, many families in the United States moved west. Some became ranchers. Ranchers needed a way to keep their ranch animals in one place. Other people in the West had farms. How could ranchers make sure their animals didn't touch farm crops?

Joseph Glidden observed that animals didn't like touching plants and shrubs that had thorns. Could this idea help keep animals in one place? Joseph tried adding sharp bits of metal, or barbs, to wire. The wire felt like it had thorns. Joseph tied this barbed wire around animal pens. It worked! It kept animals penned inside.

Ellen Ochoa (oh-CHOH-uh)

We use our sense of sight to understand things around us. When we look at something, our eyes tell us about it. Is it the same as other things we see? Or is it different?

Ellen Ochoa invented a machine that works like our eyes. This machine can look at things and tell if they are the same or different. It can spot mistakes as products are being made. Then the mistakes can be fixed.

Three years after Ochoa invented this machine, NASA chose her as an astronaut.

What can Mother Nature show you? Think about what you see, hear, taste, touch, or smell. Can you get an idea from nature? You might think up the next big invention!

What Do You Think?

How can observing things in nature help scientists get ideas?

Tracking a Storm

by Cody McCalister
illustrated by Karen Lee

Hector and Clint lived across the road from each other for many years. But last summer Clint's dad switched jobs, and his family moved to Texas. The boys stay in touch with e-mail.

File   Edit   View   Favorites   Tools   Help

To: Clint
Subject: Storm

Clint,

I just watched a news report with Mom and Dad. It showed that a big storm might hit the Texas coast. It said the storm is growing. What's the weather like near you?

My teacher this year is Mister Bennett. How's your new school?

Hector

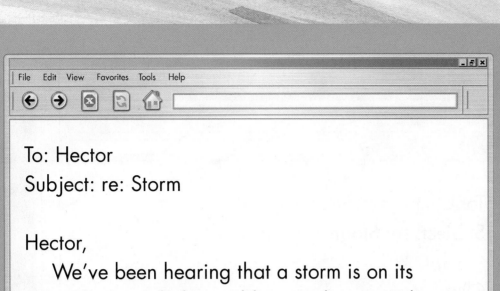

To: Hector
Subject: re: Storm

Hector,

    We've been hearing that a storm is on its way. There might be problems with rain and blowing wind. Dad said we'd have to leave and take shelter when the storm gets closer. Right now, there is still sunshine.

    School is OK, but we get a lot of homework. My teacher's name is Miss Lopez. She seems nice.

Clint

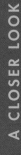

To: Clint
Subject: re: Storm

Clint,

The morning news had another report about the storm. It doesn't seem to be slowing down! I checked it out on the Web too. Did the storm get a lot closer overnight? What's the latest?

Hector

To: Hector
Subject: re: Storm

Hector,

The storm might hit tomorrow afternoon. I can feel the wind picking up, and I can taste sea air. Soon we're going inland. We'll stay with family friends.

My dog Flash will stay with our neighbor Mister Dean. Mister Dean is staying home during the storm. He's seen storms like this before.

This weekend should be something!

Clint

To: Clint
Subject: re: Storm

Clint,

I don't know when you'll read this, but I just had to write. It looks like the storm just came on shore about 50 miles north of your city. I hope everyone is OK.

Hector

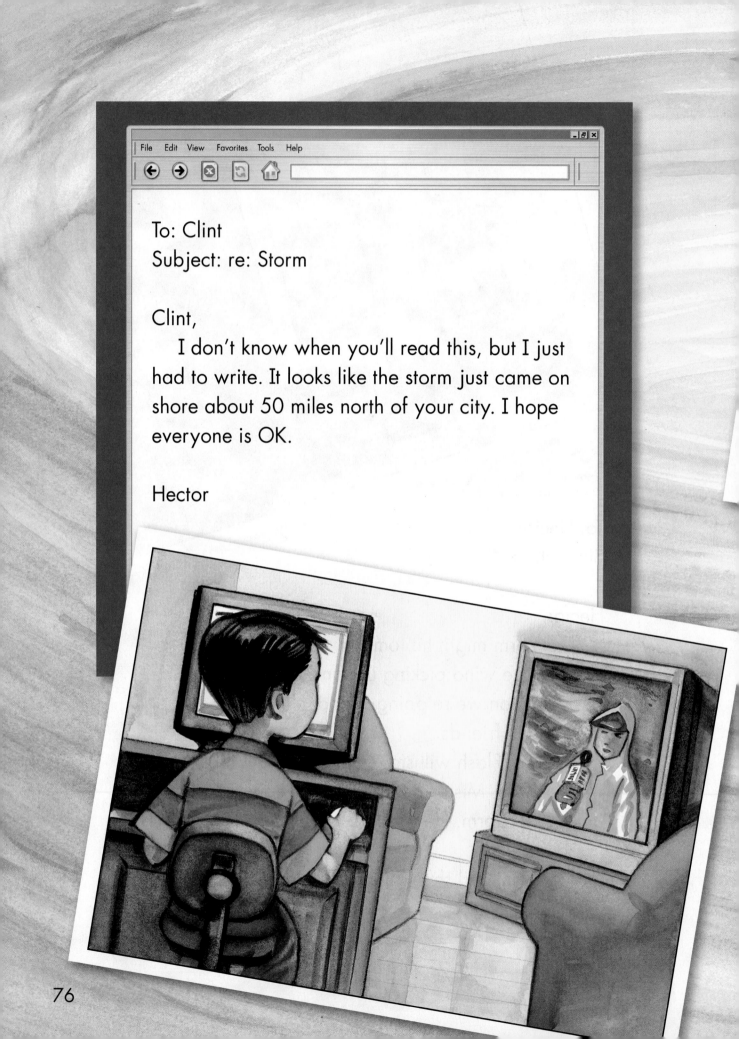

To: Hector
Subject: re: Storm

Hector,

   I'm online at the place where we're staying. We've been watching TV all day too. It looks pretty bad where the storm hit. Dad thinks our home might be OK, but we haven't been able to get in touch with Mister Dean. I'm worried about Flash. Flash hates storms.

Clint

To: Clint
Subject: re: Storm

Clint,

The news reports have shown some people returning home. Are you home yet?

Hector

To: Hector
Subject: re: Storm

Hector,

We're home. There are branches scattered in our backyard, and a funny smell is coming up from our basement. Water got in during the storm. It sure feels hot in here.

Mister Dean said Flash ran away right after the storm. But he came back. He sure was a sight for sore eyes!

Clint

What Do You Think?

Why did Clint's family go inland before the storm hit?

How to Be a

Observing birds can be fun. Here are some things you might do.

- Go someplace that birds like. This might be a park, a pond, or even your backyard.

- Use binoculars if you have them. They will give you a closer look at the birds.

- Use a bird book to help you name each bird.

- Keep a list of all the birds you see.

Bird Watcher

Here are two hints to remember.

- If you start feeding birds, keep it up. The birds will depend on you.
- When you watch birds, don't ever disturb their nests.

Invite a Bird to Lunch

- Find a pinecone.
- Tie a string around the wide end.
- Spread peanut butter over the cone.
- Roll it in birdseeds.
- Hang the pinecone from a tree.
- Watch the birds get a closer look!

4YOU2Do

Word Play

Make compound words using these words.

some	every	sun	thing	side
work	shine	light	in	home
one	out	body	land	house

Making Connections

Scientists get ideas for inventions from nature. Now it's your turn to make up an invention. Use an idea from nature. Draw a picture of your invention and write about it.

On Paper

Think of a place you like and pretend you're there. Then write what you would see, hear, smell, feel, and taste while visiting there. Can anyone guess the place you wrote about?

Possible answers for Word Play: someone, somebody, something, everyone, everybody, everything, sunshine, sunlight, inside, inland, outside, workout, homework, homeland, lighthouse, household

TO THE RESCUE!

Contents

TO THE RESCUE!

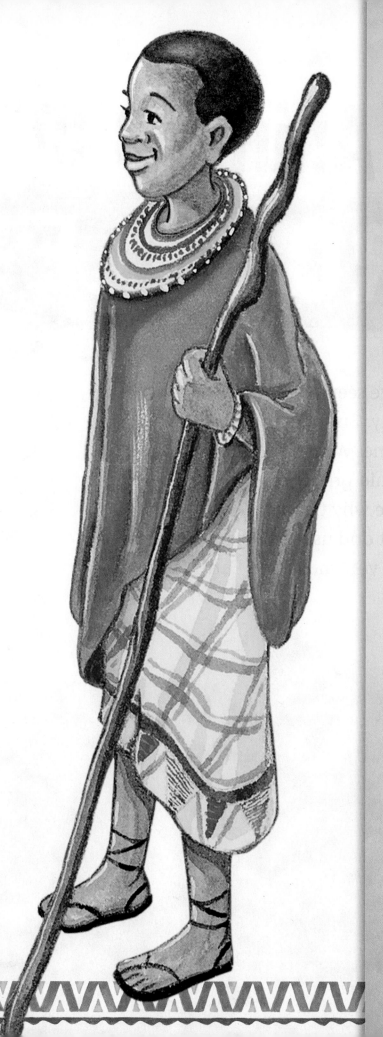

Words 2 the Wise

Some animals struggle to survive. As you read, look for ways that people come **to the rescue.**

Let's Explore

Animals in TROUBLE

You may have seen a picture of a California grizzly. But no person today will ever see a live one. Why not? It is extinct. The last California grizzly died in 1922.

It is no puzzle why this grizzly is extinct. People hunted it and used up its land. Now this animal has vanished from Earth forever.

A condor soars through the air above the Sierra Madre Mountains in California.

The California condor is endangered. That means that few condors are living today. Many of these big birds used to live in the wild. But then people settled near condors' homes. The condors had no place to nest and bring up their young. Also, condors often ate parts of animals killed by hunters. Gunshot left in those animals made the condors get sick and die.

Dark California condors with numbered tags

By the 1980s, condors had almost vanished. The outlook for them was grim.* But then animal experts tackled the problem. They made a plan to rescue the condors. They decided to trap the wild condors and bring them to a safe place. If the condors could survive in this safe place, their numbers might grow. Then some condors could return to the wild.

*grim not hopeful

The experts' plan seems to be working. Today there are about 250 condors. About half of them live in the wild.

Will you be able to see a California condor? Maybe one day. One thing is sure. Seeing this great bird up in the sky is much better than seeing a picture of it.

Rules to Protect

by Julie Lavender

This bundle of fur is a sea otter pup. Don't you just want to cuddle it? At one time, this perky little creature was almost extinct. Back in the 1700s, people hunted sea otters for their furry skins, or pelts. These pelts were soft and beautiful. They would sell for a lot of money. But in their rush to get rich, people killed far too many sea otters. In time, most sea otters had vanished.

Animals

In 1911, some countries decided to protect endangered sea otters. Leaders of these lands met and discussed how to handle the problem. First, they agreed on a set of rules. Then they signed a treaty,* the Fur Seal Treaty. This treaty said that people could not hunt sea otters. Thanks to this treaty, sea otters are not extinct today.

treaty a promise countries make to one another that says what they will or will not do

Today many countries try to protect endangered animals and plants. In fact, 169 countries signed a treaty called CITES (SYT-eez). This treaty has rules that limit trade, or buying and selling, in endangered live animals and plants. This treaty also limits trade in plant and animal parts and in things made from plants and animals.

Police in Thailand find elephant tusks at an airport. Someone was trying to smuggle, or sneak, them out of the country.

The elephant is an animal that CITES is helping. Countries that belong to CITES will not let people buy or sell elephant tusks. By stopping this trade, it is hoped that fewer elephants will be killed for their tusks. Then more elephants will survive.

Elephants at Risk

- The number of elephants in Africa is shrinking. There are just 400,000 to 600,000 elephants in Africa today. That is less than half as many as in 1979.

- People are the main reason elephants are in danger. Hunters kill elephants for their tusks. People settle on their land and drive them away.

CITES also helps tigers. Tigers are endangered because people killed them for sport and for their parts. But now CITES has a rule that forbids killing these big cats. Can this rule keep tigers from vanishing? Some people will not follow rules. One person tried to smuggle a tiger skin into another country. Someone was able to stop that crime. But it was too late to rescue that tiger.

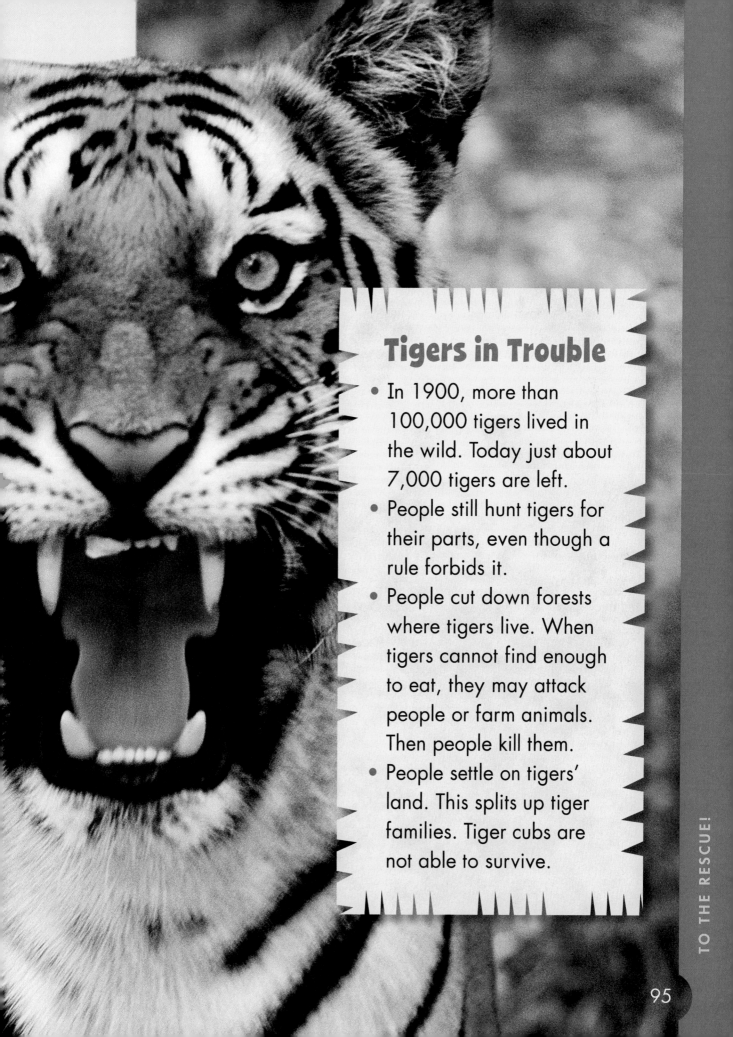

Tigers in Trouble

- In 1900, more than 100,000 tigers lived in the wild. Today just about 7,000 tigers are left.
- People still hunt tigers for their parts, even though a rule forbids it.
- People cut down forests where tigers live. When tigers cannot find enough to eat, they may attack people or farm animals. Then people kill them.
- People settle on tigers' land. This splits up tiger families. Tiger cubs are not able to survive.

Remember that furry sea otter pup? It is not extinct because people made rules to protect it. Rules are helping rescue elephants and tigers too. But many animals are still at risk.

Can you do anything to help rescue them? One simple step is to write a letter. You can write to a leader in the country where the endangered animal lives. Tell why that animal must be protected. Then one day CITES members may pass a rule to protect that animal. Perhaps one more animal will not vanish from Earth.

What Do You Think?

Should countries work together to protect animals? Why or why not?

Kisham and the Elephants

by Jelani Brown • illustrated by Gary Torrisi

"Kisham, go check on the cattle," said Father.

Father's words startled Kisham. He had been thinking about the wild elephants that roam the land. Where were they now? How he wished that he could see one.

Kisham ran up the hill, his feet kicking up dust. Where were Father's cattle? Then he spotted them. The herd had moved to find more grass to eat.

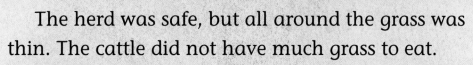

The herd was safe, but all around the grass was thin. The cattle did not have much grass to eat.

Just then Kisham heard a high burst, like a bugle. It seemed to come from nearby.

"Elephants!" he cried. Kisham turned and ran down the hill. Maybe he would get his wish. Maybe he would see an elephant today.

Kisham ran to his father, who seemed upset.

"Go away! Get off my land!" Father yelled at the elephants that trampled his grass. He waved his stick.

"But they are so grand, Father," Kisham gasped.

"Yes, elephants are grand," Father replied. "But if they trample the little bit of grass that is left on my land, my cattle will not be able to eat."

That night Kisham dreamed of elephants padding through thick green grass.

The next morning, as Kisham dressed, he heard a distant blast. Then he heard it again. "Gunfire," Kisham whispered to himself. He raced outside.

"Father!" Kisham called. "Come quick! I think the elephants may be in danger!"

Kisham and his father followed the dusty elephant tracks. They found the spot where the elephants had stopped to take a mud bath. They passed a little tree the elephants had toppled over. Then they found it.

The huge beast lay on its side in the dirt, as still as a rock. Flies buzzed around its head and tail. There were two white stumps where its two tusks had been.

"No!" Kisham cried.

"Hunters," Father grumbled. "This is their doing. They killed this elephant and stole its tusks."

Kisham looked at the two white stumps. He pictured men with rifles loading the tusks into a jeep. He pictured men selling the tusks at a big market.

Just then a soft rumble broke through the hush. "Look, Father!" Kisham cried.

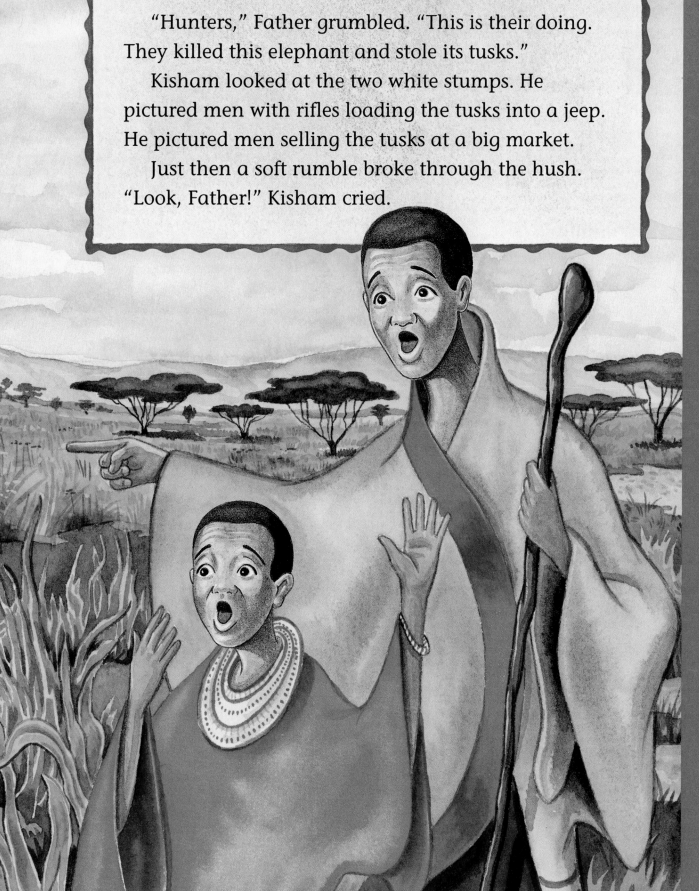

103

A baby elephant with big eyes and floppy ears was rubbing its trunk against the body in the dirt.

"A baby elephant!" Kisham cried. "We must rescue it, Father. It will not survive by itself."

Father patted Kisham on the back. "Yes, we must help," he said. "We will keep following the tracks in the dust. Perhaps they will lead us to this little one's family."

They traveled for miles. At last they found the elephants standing in the shade of a big tree. This time Father did not yell or wave his stick at the huge beasts. This time he just watched the baby elephant go back to its herd.

What Do You Think?

Did Father feel the same as Kisham about the elephants? Tell how each one felt.

Gone...but Not Forgotten

Hundreds of animals are now extinct.
These are some of them. No one knows
which animal will be next.

Carolina Parakeet
Extinct: 1920

Quagga
Extinct: 1883

N

Steller's Sea Cow
Extinct: 1768

People take over land and cut down forests. Then animals have fewer places to live. People add waste to the air and water. That makes animals sick. People hunt animals. Then animals cannot grow up and produce new young. As animals become extinct, new animals are not taking their place.

Tasmanian Tiger
Extinct: 1930s

Giant Moa
Extinct: 1600s

Dodo
Extinct: 1681

4 you 2 Do

Word Play

Make a word web for *extinct* and another for *endangered*. Work with a partner. Add words and categories to the webs. How big can your word webs get? Which web is bigger?

Making Connections

Why did Kisham and his father and the members of CITES take steps to protect animals?

On Paper

Kisham and his father saved the baby elephant by returning it to its herd. Many countries have helped animals by making rules to protect them. What could people in your community do to help endangered animals?

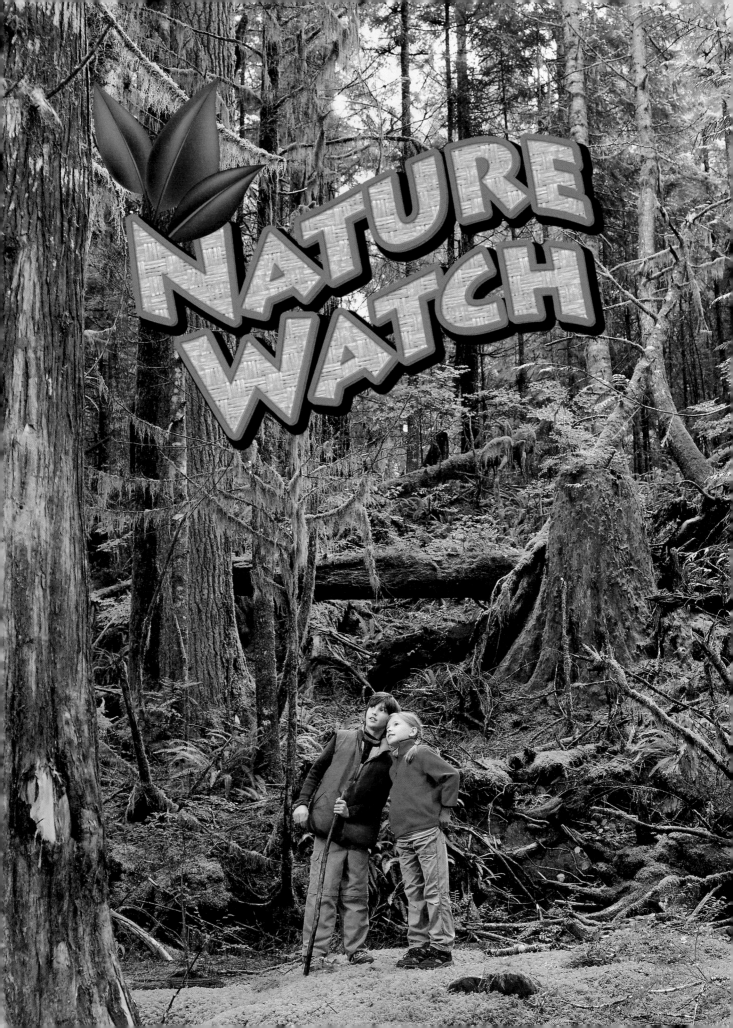

NATURE WATCH

Contents

Nature Watch

Let's Explore

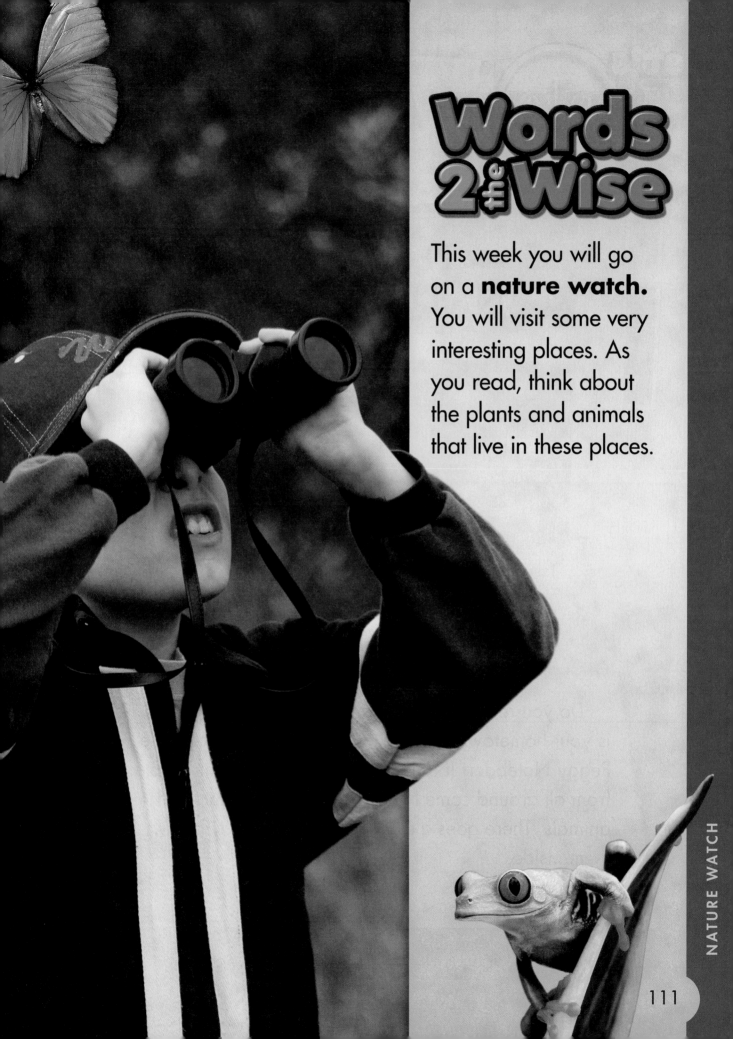

Words 2 the Wise

This week you will go on a **nature watch.** You will visit some very interesting places. As you read, think about the plants and animals that live in these places.

A Nature Center

THE PEGGY NOTEBAERT NATURE MUSEUM

Do you recognize this place? You might if Chicago is your hometown. This beautiful downtown spot is the Peggy Notebaert (NOHT-bart) Nature Museum. People from all around come here to learn about plants and animals. There goes a class of kids now! Let's follow them inside.

In this display, you can see plants and animals
in their natural surroundings. Look! A brown animal
is munching on a flower. Is it a groundhog? Listen!
Something is making a howling sound. Is it the wind?

Step up and take a closer look. Then be still and
listen. You are bound to learn something new about the
plants and animals that inhabit this place.

Flutter, flutter! Look up. Look down. You can count on seeing butterflies inside the Butterfly Haven. This greenhouse is home to hundreds of butterflies from all around the globe.

Look! A butterfly has landed on a flower. Watch as it feeds. Then hold out your hand. It might land on you next!

The fun is not just inside. There is plenty to see and do outdoors as well.

Want to go for a hike? You can take a trail through these high grasses. See bees buzz from flower to flower. Watch as spiders spin their webs.

Nature centers make for a fun trip. Why not see if one is in your hometown!

Wetlands and Rain Forests

by Karen Sandoval

When you step outdoors, what do you see? Probably not a wetland or a rain forest! Not many people know these wet places as home. But lots of plants and animals do. Let's take a closer look at these two wet, wild, and wonderful places.

Wetlands

Squish, squish! What is making that sound? Look down. It's your feet! The ground is wet here because this is a wetland. In a wetland, the ground is soaked or covered with water much of the time. Swamps, marshes, and bogs are kinds of wetlands.

This swamp is a wetland.

Splish, splash, kerplunk! What was that flash of green? You may recognize a frog. But do you know which other animals inhabit a wetland? Just look around. A playful otter dives for fish. A bird hunts from above as a snake slithers down below. A doe grazes. A lonely bobcat prowls at dusk. For these animals, this place is their natural home.

A wetland is home to many different animals.

This water lily is a wetland plant.

Wetland plants like lots of water. But did you know that many of these plants live right in the water? Beautiful flowers rise up over green lily pads. Long, thin reeds poke through the water's surface. Everything is very green.

Rain Forests

Drip, drip, drip! Now, what is that? That is the sound of water dripping in a rain forest. A rain forest is very green because it rains almost every day.

Some of Earth's highest trees grow in a rain forest. They stand more than 200 feet high. Their thick leaves block the sun. This makes it dark close to the ground.

Many strange and beautiful animals live in rain forests.

A rain forest is home to many animals. But you have to look up. Many of them live in the trees! Colorful red and green parrots perch high above ground. Odd frogs hop from one tree to the next.

Z-z-z-zap! What can that be? An eel just zapped a fish with a shock. Eels live in the muddy waters of the rain forest. Huge turtles swim there too.

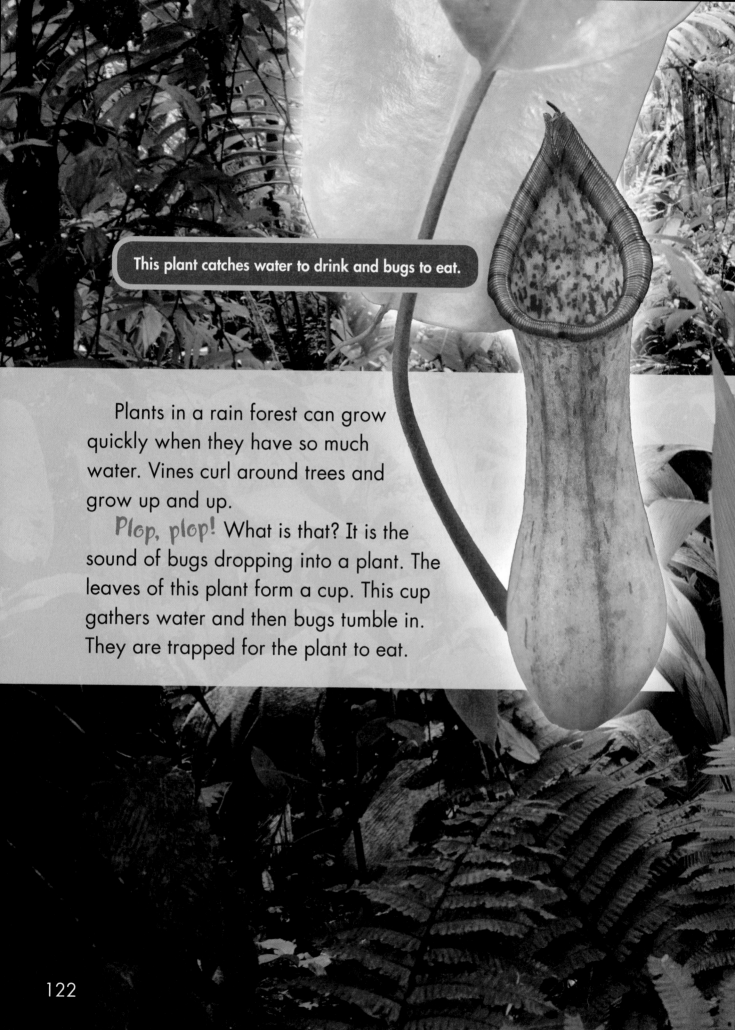

This plant catches water to drink and bugs to eat.

Plants in a rain forest can grow quickly when they have so much water. Vines curl around trees and grow up and up.

Plop, plop! What is that? It is the sound of bugs dropping into a plant. The leaves of this plant form a cup. This cup gathers water and then bugs tumble in. They are trapped for the plant to eat.

What animals do you see where you live? What plants grow around your home? They may not be what you would find in a wetland or a rain forest. But step outdoors and look closely. You may find some surprises!

What Do You Think?

How are a wetland and a rain forest the same? How are they different?

Ben's Outdoor Adventures

by Kenneth Lee
illustrated by Andy Elkerton

Ben zipped his bag shut. "OK, Dad, I'm all packed!"

"Wonderful," said Dad. "But our camping trip might need to wait a day. See those dark clouds? A storm is moving toward the campground."

Ben sat down at the computer. His bright smile quickly turned to a frown.

"Now, don't pout," said Dad. "I have a plan."

After dinner, Ben and Dad set up the tent in their backyard. "What a great idea, Dad!" Ben said. "Camping outdoors in our own backyard! Will we see animals?"

Dad chuckled. "There are animals. But most likely we'll hear them rather than see them."

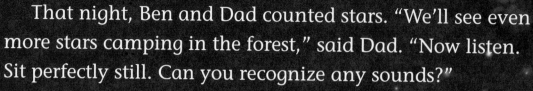

That night, Ben and Dad counted stars. "We'll see even more stars camping in the forest," said Dad. "Now listen. Sit perfectly still. Can you recognize any sounds?"

Honk, honk! Screech! Arf! Arf! Arf!

Ben listened closely. "That's a truck's horn and screeching brakes. I think it woke up that dog!"

Dad smiled. "We won't hear those sounds in the forest."

Suddenly there was a new sound. *MEOW*!
Ben jumped as a purring brown cat rubbed up against him.
"I don't think we'll hear Brownie in the forest either!"
Dad joked.

The next morning, Ben and Dad packed up the van and drove a long way. Finally they reached the campground.

Green grass and towering hills surrounded them. "This place is so beautiful," Ben whispered. Then he shouted, "Look, Dad!" A doe bounded past them.

"This is its natural environment, Ben," Dad said. "Many animals inhabit the forest."

That night, Ben and Dad sat by the campfire. "It's so dark," said Ben. "I can see so many stars."

"Can you recognize any sounds?" Dad asked. "Listen."
At first, the forest seemed quiet. Then . . .

Ribbit, ribbit! Chirp, chirp, chirp! Crackle, pop!

"I hear frogs and bugs and our campfire!" said Ben.

CHIRP!

RIBBIT!

POP!

CHIRP!

WHO!

Then Ben heard a new sound.
Who! Who! Who!
"Wh-wh-what is that?" Ben asked.
"That's just an owl, Ben," Dad
said. "Owls come out at night. They're
not harmful."

The next day, Ben and Dad started to pack up. Not far away, there was a flash and a rumble of thunder. They turned to look. The sky was filling with dark clouds.

"Now *that's* a sound I know," said Ben.

"It means it's time to go home!"

What Do You Think?
How was camping in the backyard and in the forest the same? How was it different?

131

Backyard Wildlife

Would you like to watch butterflies, birds, and other animals up close? Kids across the country are creating wildlife habitats at home—in backyards, on balconies, and outside windows. You too can make your home a welcome place for wildlife. Just follow these tips.

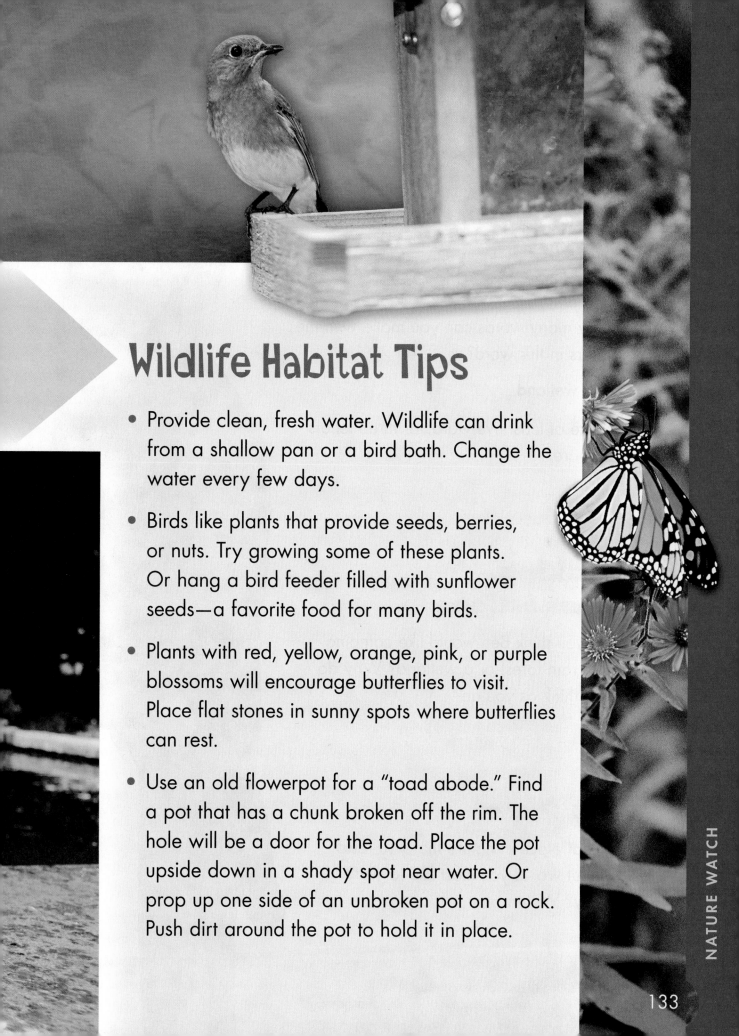

Wildlife Habitat Tips

- Provide clean, fresh water. Wildlife can drink from a shallow pan or a bird bath. Change the water every few days.

- Birds like plants that provide seeds, berries, or nuts. Try growing some of these plants. Or hang a bird feeder filled with sunflower seeds—a favorite food for many birds.

- Plants with red, yellow, orange, pink, or purple blossoms will encourage butterflies to visit. Place flat stones in sunny spots where butterflies can rest.

- Use an old flowerpot for a "toad abode." Find a pot that has a chunk broken off the rim. The hole will be a door for the toad. Place the pot upside down in a shady spot near water. Or prop up one side of an unbroken pot on a rock. Push dirt around the pot to hold it in place.

4 you 2 Do

Word Play

How many words can you make with the letters in this word?

wetland

Make at least five words of three letters or more.

Making Connections

Do you think Ben would like camping in a rain forest or a wetland? Why do you think as you do?

On Paper

What place in nature that you read about would you most like to visit? Why? Write about it.

Possible answers for Word Play: wet, land, tan, and, net, tend, dew, ten, wand, den, neat, deal

beau • ti • ful (byü′ tə fəl), *ADJECTIVE.* very pleasing to see or hear; delighting the mind or senses: *After the rain stopped, it became a beautiful, sunny day.* **beau•ti•ful•ly.**

dis • cov • er (dis kuv′ ər), *VERB.* to find out something that was not known before: *He discovered tiny insects living under the stone.* **dis•cov•ered, dis•cov•er•ing.**

el • e • phant (el′ ə fənt), *NOUN.* a very large mammal: *An elephant has large ears and a long trunk.*

en • dan • gered (en dān′ jərd), ADJECTIVE. at risk of no longer existing: *Giant pandas are endangered animals.*

ex • plain (ek splān′), VERB. to tell about something so that people are able to understand it: *The teacher explained multiplication to the class.* **ex•plained, ex•plain•ing.**

ex • tinct (ek stingkt′), ADJECTIVE. no longer existing: *Dinosaurs are extinct.*

a in hat	ō in open	sh in she
ā in age	ȯ in all	th in thin
â in care	ô in order	ŦH in then
ä in far	oi in oil	zh in measure
e in let	ou in out	⌈ a in about
ē in equal	u in cup	⎢ e in taken
ėr in term	ù in put	ə = ⎨ i in pencil
i in it	ü in rule	⎢ o in lemon
ī in ice	ch in child	⌊ u in circus
o in hot	ng in long	

flow • er (flou′ ər), *NOUN.* a part of a plant or tree that
produces the seed; blossom: *My favorite flower is a tulip.*

grow (grō), *VERB.* to become bigger: *Plants grow from seeds.*
grew, grow•ing, grown.

in • hab • it (in hab′ it), *VERB.* to live in: *Fish inhabit the sea.*
in•hab•it•ed, in•hab•it•ing.

myth (mith), *NOUN.* a legend or story, usually one that attempts to explain something in nature: *According to Greek myth, the god Zeus used lightning as a weapon.*

nat•ur•al (nach′ ər əl), *ADJECTIVE.* not artificial; not made by human beings: *Coal and oil are natural products.*

na•ture (nā′ chər), *NOUN.* everything in the world not made by people: *Plants, animals, air, water, mountains, and people are parts of nature.*

a in hat	ō in open	sh in she
ā in age	ȯ in all	th in thin
â in care	ô in order	ᵀH in then
ä in far	oi in oil	zh in measure
e in let	ou in out	⌈ a in about
ē in equal	u in cup	e in taken
ėr in term	ù in put	ə = ⟨ i in pencil
i in it	ü in rule	o in lemon
ī in ice	ch in child	⌊ u in circus
o in hot	ng in long	

ob•serve (əb zėrv′), *VERB.* to look at something carefully in order to learn about it; study: *Astronomers observe the stars.* **ob•served, ob•serv•ing.**

out•doors (out′ dôrz′),
1 *ADVERB.* outside; not indoors: *Let's go outdoors to play ball.*
2 *NOUN.* the world outside; the open air: *Let's have a day of hiking in the great outdoors.*

rec•og•nize (rek′əg nīz), *VERB.* to realize that you have seen or known someone or something before: *You have grown so much that I hardly recognized you.* **rec•og•niz•ed, rec•og•niz•ing.**

res•cue (res′ kyü), *VERB.* to save someone or something from danger, capture, or harm; free; deliver: *The dog was rescued from danger.* **res•cued, res•cu•ing.**

scat • ter (skat′ ər), VERB. to throw a little bit of something here and some more over there; sprinkle: *Let's scatter salt on the sidewalk to melt the ice.* **scat•tered, scat•ter•ing.**

sci • en • tist (sī′ ən tist), NOUN. a person who studies a science: *A scientist tries to find out why things are the way they are.*

sens • es (sens′ iz), PL. NOUN. the powers of a living thing to know what happens outside itself; sight, smell, taste, hearing, and touch are the physical senses: *A dog has very good senses of hearing and smell.*

a	in hat	ō	in open	sh	in she
ā	in age	ȯ	in all	th	in thin
â	in care	ô	in order	ᵀH	in then
ä	in far	oi	in oil	zh	in measure
e	in let	ou	in out		⎧ a in about
ē	in equal	u	in cup		⎪ e in taken
ėr	in term	u̇	in put	ə =	⎨ i in pencil
i	in it	ü	in rule		⎪ o in lemon
ī	in ice	ch	in child		⎩ u in circus
o	in hot	ng	in long		

sight (sīt), *NOUN.*
> 1 the power or sense of seeing: *We know what things look like through our sense of sight.*
>
> 2 thing seen; view; glimpse: *I can't stand the sight of blood.*

soil (soil), *NOUN.* the top layer of the Earth; dirt: *They planted flowers in rich soil.*

taste (tāst),
> 1 *NOUN.* the power to take in the flavor that things have: *The taste of sugar is sweet.*
>
> 2 *VERB.* to find out whether something is sweet, sour, salty, or bitter when you put it in your mouth: *You taste things with your tongue.* **tast·ed, tast·ing.**

touch (tuch),

> 1 *NOUN.* the power by which a person knows about things by feeling or handling them: *Touch is one of the five senses.*
> 2 *VERB.* to be next to; come up against: *Your sleeve is touching the butter.* **touched, touch·ing.**

van·ish (van′ ish), *VERB.* to disappear suddenly: *The sun vanished behind a cloud.* **van·ished, van·ish·ing.**

veg·e·ta·ble (vej′ tə bəl or vej′ ə tə bəl), *NOUN.* a plant that has fruit, seeds, leaves, roots, or other parts used for food: *Peas, lettuce, beets, and zucchini are vegetables.*

a in hat	ō in open	sh in she
ā in age	o̊ in all	th in thin
â in care	ô in order	ᴛ̅ʜ in then
ä in far	oi in oil	zh in measure
e in let	ou in out	⎡ a in about
ē in equal	u in cup	⎢ e in taken
ėr in term	u̇ in put	ə = ⎨ i in pencil
i in it	ü in rule	⎢ o in lemon
ī in ice	ch in child	⎣ u in circus
o in hot	ng in long	

Acknowledgments

Text

Every effort has been made to locate the copyright owner of material reproduced in this component. Omissions brought to our attention will be corrected in subsequent editions. Grateful acknowledgment is made to the following for copyrighted material.

28 Chez Panisse Foundation c/o The Edible Schoolyard "Recipe for Frittata" from *http://www.edibleschoolyard.org/frittata.html.* Copyright © 2006–2009 The Edible Schoolyard. Used by permission of Chez Panisse Foundation c/o The Edible Schoolyard.

Illustrations

20–26 Mercedes McDonald; **28, 29** Patt Dalby; **34, 36** Beatrice Willey; **36** Robert (Bob) Kayganich; **38** Matt Zang; **54** Felipe Ugalde; **60–63** Laura Freeman-Hines; **72–79** Karen Jones Lee; **86, 98–104** Gary Torrisi; **106** Steven Mach; **110, 124–131** Andy Elkerton.

Photographs

Every effort has been made to secure permission and provide appropriate credit for photographic material. The publisher deeply regrets any omission and pledges to correct errors called to its attention in subsequent editions.

Unless otherwise acknowledged, all photographs are the property of Pearson Education, Inc.

Photo locators denoted as follows: Top (T), Center (C), Bottom (B), Left (L), Right (R), Background (Bkgd)

Cover: (BR) ©WizData, Inc./Alamy, (C) Frans Lanting/Minden Pictures, (CL) Getty Images, (BL) Jim Boorman/Jupiter Images; **1** (CL, BL) Kenneth Garrett/National Geographic Image Collection; **2** (BL) ©Annie Griffiths Belt/Corbis, (TR) ©Stockbyte, (CL) Robert Pickett/Alamy Images; **3** (BR) ©Sigrid Dauth (Travel Germany 2005)/Alamy Images, (BR) Getty Images, (T) Tom Vezo/Nature Picture Library; **5** (C, BL) ©Royalty-Free/Corbis; **6** (TR) ©Stockbyte; **7** (BR) ©WizData, Inc./Alamy; **8** (TR) ©Stockbyte, (C) Sean Justice/Getty Images; **9** (CR) Tom Stewart/Corbis; **10** (BL) Todd Gipstein/National Geographic Image Collection; **11** (BR) ©WizData, Inc./Alamy, (T) Dennis Frates/Alamy Images; **13** (C) Mary Evans Picture Library/Alamy Images; **14** (C) ©Gianni Dagli Orti/Corbis; **15** ©Burton Zaro/Alamy Images; **16** (C) Robert C. Lautman/Thomas Jefferson Foundation, Inc.; **17** (C) Robert C. Lautman/Thomas Jefferson Foundation, Inc.; **18** (CC) Chelsea Chapmen/©The Edible Schoolyard; **19** (CR) Chelsea Chapman/©The Edible Schoolyard; **28** (C) Chelsea Chapman/©The Edible Schoolyard; **31** (T, C) Getty Images; **32** (CR) Heather Angel/Alamy Images, (BR) Maximilian Weinzierl/Alamy Images, (TR) Robert Pickett/Alamy Images; **33** (BR) ©Royalty-Free/Corbis, (TL) Blickwinkel/Alamy Images; **35** (B) ©Studio Photogram/Alamy; **37** (TL) ©Pete Turner/Getty Images; **38** (C) BananaStock, (Bkgd) Richard Hamilton Smith/Corbis; **40** (TR) ©Royalty-Free/Corbis, (BR, BL) Gary Vestal/Getty Images, (Bkgd) Getty Images; **41** (CR) ©Royalty-Free/Corbis, (BR, BL) Gary Vestal/Getty Images, (Bkgd) Getty Images; **42** (Bkgd) ©Dietrich Rose/Getty Images, (CL) Getty Images, (R) Konard Zelazowski/Alamy Images; **43** (CR) Photos to Go/Photolibrary; **44** (TL) Getty Images, (BC) Jason Edwards/National Geographic Image Collection, (Bkgd) Richard Hamilton Smith/Corbis; **45** (BL) ©Darrell Gulin/Getty Images; **46** (Bkgd, B) Getty Images; **47** (C) A. Riedmiller/Peter Arnold, Inc., (Bkgd) Jupiter Images; **48** (C) Arne Pastoor/Getty Images, (Bkgd) Jupiter Images; **49** (Bkgd) Getty Images, (C) Richard T Nowitz/Corbis; **50** (B) ©Annie Griffiths Belt/Corbis, (CR) Barry Rosenthal/Getty Images, (Bkgd) Getty Images, (CL) Heather Angel/Alamy Images; **51** (TR) ©Pixtal/SuperStock; **52** (B) Brownie Harris/Corbis, (CL) Getty Images; **53** (B) ©Paul & Lindamarie Ambrose/Getty Images; **56** (TL) Blickwinkel/Alamy Images, (TC) Robert Pickett/Alamy Images, (CL) Zave Smith/Getty Images; **57** (C) Glowimages/Getty Images; **58** (TR) ©Royalty-Free/Corbis, (TCR) Getty Images, (TR) Stefano Bianchetti/Corbis; **64** (TL) Getty Images, (TL) Stefano Bianchetti/Corbis; **65** (TR) Alinari Archives/Corbis, (TR) Mary Evans/Alamy Images, (Bkgd) O. Louis Mazzatenta/Getty Images; **66** (CL) ©Bettmann/Corbis, (TR) DAJ/Getty Images, (C) Getty Images, (T) Martin Ruegner/Getty Images; **67** (C) Blend Images/Getty Images, (TR) DAJ/Getty Images, (T) Getty Images; **68** (CL) Corbis/Corbis, (TL) Getty Images, (T) Wilmar Photography/Alamy Images; **70** (T) ©Eyebyte/Alamy, (TL) NASA, (C) Stockdisc; **71** (T) Bill Bachmann/Alamy Images; **80** (TCR) Gavriel Jecan/Corbis, (TL) Joe Mcdonald/Corbis, (TCL) Joe McDonald/Corbis, (BR) Sigrid Oisson/Getty Images; **81** (TR) Arthur Morris/Corbis, (T) George D Lepp/Corbis; **82** (TL) Arthur Morris/Corbis, (BR) Getty Images; **83** (C) Thinkstock; **84** (CR) Frans Lanting/Minden Pictures; **87** (TR) C.C. Lockwood/Animals Animals/Earth Scenes, (TL) Tom Vezo/Nature Picture Library; **88** (TC) ©Tom Brownold; **89** (TL) Joel Sartore/National Geographic Image Collection, (BC) Kenneth W. Fink/Photo Researchers, Inc.; **90** (TL) ©Stuart Westmorland/Getty Images, (B) Steven J. Kazlowski/Alamy Images; **92** (CL) Sukree Sukplang/Corbis, (Bkgd) Tom Brakefield/Corbis; **93** (CL) Kenneth Garrett/National Geographic Image Collection; **94** (BL) David A. Northcutt/Corbis; **95** (CL) Frans Lanting/Corbis; **96** (BL) Frans Lanting/Minden Pictures, (TR) Steve Bloom/Alamy Images; **108** (CR) Kenneth Garrett/National Geographic Image Collection; **109** (C) ©Ryan McVay/Getty Images; **111** (T) ©ethylalkohol/Shutterstock, (BR) ©iStockphoto; **113** (C) Photolibrary; **114** (C) ©Cathleen Howland/Shutterstock; **115** (C) Courtesy of Peggy Notebaert Nature Museum, (C) Digital Stock; **116** (C) ©Horowitz, Ross M./Getty Images, (B) ©Sigrid Dauth (Travel Germany 2005)/Alamy Images; **117** (C) ©David A. Ponton/Mira, (CL) ©T.J. Rich/Nature Picture Library; **118** (C) ©David A. Ponton/Mira, (CR) ©Frans Lanting/Corbis, (C) ©Karin Duthie/Alamy Images, (BL) ©Wendy Shattil/Stock Connection; **119** (B) ©Terry Whittaker/Alamy Images, (CR) ©Wm. Baker/GhostWorx Images/Alamy Images; **120** (BR) ©Edward Parker/Alamy Images, (BL) ©ethylalkohol/Shutterstock, (CR) ©iStockphoto, (C) ©Margarette Mead/Getty Images; **121** (CR) ©Lisa F. Young/Shutterstock; **122** (CR) Photos to Go/Photolibrary, (C) ©Margarette Mead/Getty Images; **123** (BL) ©DK Images, (C) ©Susan Jones/PhotoLibrary Group, Inc.; **132** (TR) ©Michael Lustbader/Photo Researchers, Inc., (C) Photolibrary; **133** (T) ©Gary W. Carter/Corbis, (CL) ©Radius Images/Photolibrary; **134** (CR) ©Michael Klenetsky/Shutterstock; **136** (B) Kenneth Garrett/National Geographic Image Collection; **137** (B) Heather Angel/Alamy Images; **138** (B) Robert C. Lautman/Thomas Jefferson Foundation, Inc.; **139** (B) ©David A. Ponton/Mira; **140** (B) Thinkstock; **141** (TR) Getty Images; **142** (CR) Sean Justice/Getty Images; **143** (CR) Tom Stewart/Corbis.

MY SiDEWALKS ON
SCOTT FORESMAN
READING STREET

UNIT 3

PEARSON
Scott
Foresman

pearsonschool.com

ISBN-13: 978-0-328-45282-8
ISBN-10: 0-328-45282-3

EAN

9 780328 452828

90000>

Level C3

Cultures

How Cool!

They wore that?!?!

Time Travel

Explore past cultures.

Be Brave

Try new foods!